The Ice Cream Boys
by Gail Louw

Jermyn Street Theatre
9 October — 2 November, 2019

Press performance Friday 11 October

The Ice Cream Boys premiered at Jermyn Street Theatre on 9 October, 2019 with the following cast:

CAST

Jacob Zuma	Andrew Francis
Ronnie Kasrils	Jack Klaff
Thandi Dube	Bu Kunene

CREATIVE TEAM

Director	Vik Sivalingam
Set & Costume Designer	Cecilia Trono
Lighting Designer	Tim Mascall
Sound Designer	Nicola Chang
Production Co-ordinator	Jo Heanley
Stage Manager	Anna Short
Assistant Stage Manager	Kate Francis
Set Builder	James Donnelly
Videographer & Rehearsal Photographer	Anna Urik
Production Photographer	Robert Workman

Produced and general managed by Jermyn Street Theatre in association with Jeffrey T. Apter.

With thanks to Arts Council England, Max Adelman, Scott Carver and Peter Samuels.

Supported using public funding by
ARTS COUNCIL ENGLAND

CAST

JACK KLAFF | RONNIE KASRILS

For Jermyn Street Theatre: *Statements*, *Moscow Art Workshop*, *Foreign Sky* and *Ivy and Joan*.

Other theatre includes: *Macbeth*, *Cherry Orchard* (Birmingham Repertory); *Representative*, *Drama at Inish*, *Still Goes On* (Finborough); *Henry VI*, *Sons of Light*, *As You Like It*, *Tamburlaine*, *School of Night* (Royal Shakespeare Company); *Tempest*, *Botticelli* (Oxford Playhouse); *Nagging Doubt* (Donmar Warehouse); *Stockwell* (Kiln Theatre); *Matchmaker*, *Map of the Heart* (West End); *Point Vallaine* (Chichester Festival Theatre); *National Health*, *Merchant of Venice*, *Othello*, *I'm Not Rappaport*, *Letters*, *Evening Light* (Bristol Old Vic); *Oedipus*, *Cuddles*, *Secrets* (Tristan Bates); *Royal Hunt of the Sun* (National Tour); *Carver*, *Lower Depths*, *Cherry Orchard* (Arcola); *Shirleymander*, *WhoWhatWhyBus* (The Playground Theatre); *Frankenstein*, *Midsummer Night's Dream* (US Tour/New York); and *Richard II* (Rose Theatre Bankside)

Television includes: *The Sweeney*, *Miner's Strike*, *Poirot*, *Sherlock Holmes*, *Boon*, *Rendell – Road Rage*, *Last Duel*, *Vanity Fair*, *Midsomer*, *Grushko*, *Whoops Apocalypse*, *Death is Part of the Process*, *Ivanhoe*, *Cadfael* and his own solo works.

Film includes: *Star Wars*, *For Your Eyes Only*, *King David*, *1871*, *Threat*, *Storage*, *Decadentally* and *Eyes of Orson Welles*.

Radio includes: *Notre Dame*, *Brave New World*, *Phantom of the Opera*, *Tynan*, *Importance of Being Frank*, *Welles*, *With Great Pleasure*, *Poetry Please*, *Comandante* and several of his own works.

ANDREW FRANCIS | JACOB ZUMA

Theatre includes: *Comedy of Errors* (Ludlow Festival); *Romeo and Juliet* (Belgrade Theatre); *Comedy of Errors* (Nottingham Playhouse); *Master Harold and the Boys* (Palace Theatre) and *On the Death of Ken Sara-Wiwa* (Contact Theatre).

Television includes: *Doctors*, *Messiah*, *EastEnders* and *The Benny Hill Show*.

Radio includes: *Desire*, *The Woodcutter* and *London*.

BU KUNENE | THANDI DUBE

Theatre includes: *12 Angry women* (Producers Club Theatre, New York City); *A Sketch of New York* (The Alpha NYC Theatre Company) and *Harvest* (Wallis Knot Theatre Company).

Film includes: *Ear of The Beholder* and *Indigo*.

CREATIVE TEAM

GAIL LOUW | WRITER

For Jermyn Street Theatre: *Shackleton's Carpenter* (also UK Tours).

Other theatre includes: *Blonde Poison* (UK/Los Angeles/South Africa/Auckland/Wellington/Sydney/Melbourne/Berlin); *Miss Dietrich Regrets* (UK/Prague); *The Half Life of Love* (UK/Oregon); *Two Sisters* (UK/Los Angeles/Oregon); *Mitfords* (UK); *Being Brahms* (UK); *And This Is My Friend Mr Laurel* (Edinburgh/UK/Dubai); *Killing Faith*; *Joe Ho Ho*; *Duwayne*; *A Life Twice Given* and *Larkin* (UK).

Gail has had several awards including Argus Award for Artistic Excellence for *Blonde Poison*, Best New Play at Brighton Festival for *Duwayne* and Naledi Award in South Africa for *Miss Dietrich Regrets*.

VIK SIVALINGAM | DIRECTOR

Theatre includes: *There of Here* (Park Theatre); *Home* (The Last Refuge); *The Drunken City* (Tabard Theatre); *Twelfth Night* (Iris Theatre); *Macbeth*, *Wild Honey* (Sainsbury Theatre); *The Tempest* (Rio Olympics); *Invisible Man* (Royal Shakespeare Company, Park Avenue Armory, New York); *The Radio Serenade* (Medicine Show Theatre, New York); *Much Ado About Nothing* (The Whitman Theatre, New York); *In Arabia, We'd All Be Kings* (Carne Theatre); *Posh* (Greenwood Theatre); *Closer* (New Crescent Theatre); and *Crimes of the Heart* (Old Rep Theatre).

Vik is a graduate of the Arts Council/Birkbeck University of London MFA in Theatre Directing and also holds a Post Graduate Award in Teaching Shakespeare (Royal Shakespeare Company/Warwick University).

CECILIA TRONO | SET & COSTUME DESIGNER

For Jermyn Street Theatre: *The Last Ones* (OffWestEnd nomination – Best Set Designer); *Statements After an Arrest Under the Immorality Act* and *Fever* (Assistant Designer).

Design credits include: *Mites* (Tristan Bates); *The Curious Case of Benjamin Button*, *The Rubenstein Kiss* (Southwark Playhouse); *The Paradise Circus* (The Playground Theatre); *The Blue Hour of Natalie Barney* (Arcola); *The Riots* (Stratford Circus, London); *She is Shakespeare* (Théâtre de Ménilmontant, Paris) and *Bluebeard's Castle* in collaboration with OperaUpClose (The North Wall, Oxford).

Cecilia is a French performance designer based in London. She graduated with First Class Honours from Rose Bruford College in 2017.

TIM MASCALL | LIGHTING DESIGNER

For Jermyn Street Theatre: *Tomorrow At Noon*, *Mad As Hell*, *Tonight At 8:30*, *I Have Been Here Before*, *Bloody Poetry*, *The Autumn Garden* and *The Notorious Mrs Ebbsmith*.

Other theatre includes: *Orpheus Descending* (Theatr Clwyd/ Menier Chocolate Factory); *Lord Of The Flies* (Theatr Clwyd/ Sherman Theatre); *Midsummer* (National Theatre of Scotland); *Rails*, *Bold Girls* (Theatre by the Lake); *Jumpy*, *A Taste Of Honey*, *Long Days Journey Into Night*, *Kill Jonny Glendenning*, *Faith Healer* (Royal Lyceum, Edinburgh); *Licensed to Ill* (Cornershop); *Consent*, *The Truth*, *A Little Night Music*, *My Fair Lady*, *Who's Afraid of Virginia Woolf* (Central Theatre, Budapest); *Without You*, *Breakfast With Jonny Wilkinson*, *Fully Committed* (Menier Chocolate Factory); *The Maids* (Dundee Rep); *The Real Thing* (Bath Theatre Royal); *Pygmalion* (English Theatre Frankfurt); *I Loved Lucy* (Arts Theatre); *Why The Whales Came* (Harold Pinter Theatre); *The Vagina Monologues* (Wyndham's); *Eric and Little Ern*, *Potted Panto* (Vaudeville); *Invincible* (St. James); *Derren Brown: Miracle, Infamous*

(Palace Theatre); *Something Wicked This Way Comes* (Old Vic); *Enigma* (Adelphi); *Evening Of Wonder*, *Potted Potter* (Garrick); and *Ruby Wax: Losing It* (Duchess).

Opera credits include: *Peter Grimes*, *The Gamblers* (LPO at the Royal Festival Hall); *Aida* (Opera Holland Park) and *The Cunning Little Vixen* (Garsington).

NICOLA CHANG | SOUND DESIGNER

Theatre includes: *Little Baby Jesus*, *The Tempest* (Orange Tree); *Wild Goose Dreams* (Ustinov Studio, Bath Theatre Royal); *Germ Free Adolescent* (Bunker Theatre); *The King of Hell's Palace* (Hampstead); *The Death of Ophelia* (Sam Wanamaker Playhouse, Shakespeare's Globe); *Wonder Winterland* (Oxford School of Drama/Soho Theatre); *Summer Rolls* (Park Theatre); *White Pearl* (Royal Court); *Trying to Find Me* (PULSE Festival/Latitude); *From Shore to Shore* (Manchester Royal Exchange/UK Tour); *Lord of the Flies* (Greenwich Theatre); *Pool (no water)* (Oxford School of Drama/Royal Court); *No Man's Land* (Square Chapel, Halifax); *Dangerous Giant Animals* (Tristan Bates); *Finishing the Picture* (Finborough); *A Hundred Words for Snow* (Arcola); *10*, *Kompromat*, *Inside Voices* (VAULT 2019); and *The Free9* (National Theatre).

JERMYN STREET THEATRE

Jermyn Street Theatre is celebrating its twenty-fifth birthday this year.

During the 1930s, the basement of 16b Jermyn Street – close to Piccadilly in the heart of London's West End – was home to the glamorous Monseigneur Restaurant and Club. The space was converted into a theatre by Howard Jameson and Penny Horner in the early 1990s, and Jermyn Street Theatre staged its first production in August 1994. The theatre director Neil Marcus became the first Artistic Director in 1995 and secured Lottery funding for the venue; the producer Chris Grady also made a major contribution to the theatre's development. In the late 1990s, the Artistic Director was David Babani, later the founder and Artistic Director of the Menier Chocolate Factory.

Over the last twenty-five years, the theatre has established itself as one of London's leading Off-West End studio theatres, with hit productions including *Barefoot in the Park* with Alan Cox and Rachel Pickup, directed by Sally Hughes, and *Helping Harry* with Adrian Lukis and Simon Dutton, directed by Nickolas Grace.

Gene David Kirk, accompanied by Associate Director Anthony Biggs, became Artistic Director in the late 2000s and reshaped the theatre's creative output with revivals of rarely performed plays, including Charles Morgan's post-war classic *The River Line*, the UK premiere of Ibsen's first performed play *St John's Night*, and another Ibsen, *Little Eyolf* starring Imogen Stubbs and Doreen Mantle. Tom Littler staged two acclaimed Stephen Sondheim revivals: *Anyone Can Whistle*, starring Issy van Randwyck and Rosalie Craig, and *Saturday Night*, which transferred to the Arts Theatre.

In 2012, Trevor Nunn directed the world premiere of Samuel Beckett's radio play *All That Fall*, starring Eileen Atkins and Michael Gambon. The production subsequently transferred to the Arts Theatre and then to New York's 59E59 Theatre. Jermyn Street Theatre was nominated for the Peter Brook Empty Space Award in 2011 and won The Stage 100 Best Fringe Theatre in 2012. Anthony Biggs became Artistic Director in 2013, combining his love of rediscoveries with a new focus on emerging artists and writers from outside the UK. Revivals included Eugene O'Neill's early American work *The First Man*, Terence Rattigan's first play *First Episode*, John Van Druten's First World War drama *Flowers of the Forest*, and a repertory season of South African drama. New works include US playwright Ruby Rae Spiegel's *Dry Land*, Jonathan Lewis's *A Level Playing Field*, and Sarah Daniels' *Soldiers' Wives* starring Cath Shipton.

In 2017, Jermyn Street Theatre started a bold new chapter, becoming the West End's newest and smallest producing theatre. Under the leadership of Artistic Director and Executive Producer Tom Littler, a small in-house producing team create or co-produce all the theatre's productions. Partnerships have been forged with numerous regional theatres including English Theatre Frankfurt, Guildford Shakespeare Company, the Stephen Joseph Theatre, Theatre by the Lake, Theatre Royal Bath, the Watermill Theatre, and York Theatre Royal.

Jermyn Street Theatre's first two years as a producing theatre have seen six seasons of work: the Escape, Scandal, Reaction, Rebels, Portrait and Memories Seasons. These have included fifteen world premieres, European premieres of American drama,

several major rediscoveries, Christmas comedies, and acclaimed new translations of classic plays. The theatre is committed to equal gender representation both onstage and offstage. It is also committed to paying a fair and legal wage, and has a bespoke agreement with the industry union, Equity. A Director's Circle of private donors is key to the theatre's survival and growth.

In 2018, Littler directed the most ambitious project in the theatre's history – the first complete London revival since 1936 of Noël Coward's nine-play cycle *Tonight at 8.30*. Previous Deputy Director Stella Powell-Jones brought *Tomorrow at Noon* to the stage – three contemporary responses to Coward's work by female playwrights. The two productions ran side-by-side leading to thirty-six one-act plays performed each week, with tremendously popular trilogy days on Saturdays and Sundays.

Throughout its history, the theatre's founders, Howard Jameson and Penny Horner, have continued to serve as Chair of the Board and Executive Director respectively, and the generous donors, front-of-house staff, and tireless volunteers all play their parts in the Jermyn Street Theatre story.

SUPPORT JERMYN STREET THEATRE

Everybody needs their best friends, and every theatre needs them too. At Jermyn Street Theatre we have recently started a Director's Circle. Limited to twenty-five individuals or couples, these are the people we rely on most. They sponsor productions, fund new initiatives, and support our staff. It is a pleasure to get to know them: we invite Director's Circle members to our exclusive press nights and parties, and we often have informal drinks or suppers in small groups. They are also an invaluable sounding board for me. Currently, members of the Director's Circle donate between £2,000 and £70,000 (with a threshold of £2,000 to join). They are our heroes and they make everything possible. We have space at the table for more, and I would love to hear from you.

Tom Littler
Artistic Director
tomlittler@jermynstreettheatre.co.uk

THE DIRECTORS' CIRCLE

Anonymous
Michael & Gianni Alen-Buckley
Philip & Christine Carne
Jocelyn Abbey & Tom Carney
Colin Clark
Flora Fraser
Charles Glanville & James Hogan
Marjorie Simonds-Gooding
Peter Soros & Electra Toub
Martin Ward & Frances Card
Duncan & Ros McMillan
Robert Westlake & Marit Mohn
Melanie Vere Nicoll

AT JERMYN STREET THEATRE

Find us at www.jermynstreettheatre.co.uk @JSTheatre
Box Office: 020 7287 2875
16b Jermyn Street, London SW1Y 6ST

THE ICE-CREAM BOYS

Gail Louw

THE ICE CREAM BOYS

OBERON BOOKS
LONDON

WWW.OBERONBOOKS.COM

First published in 2019 by Oberon Books Ltd
521 Caledonian Road, London N7 9RH
Tel: +44 (0) 20 7607 3637 / Fax: +44 (0) 20 7607 3629
e-mail: info@oberonbooks.com
www.oberonbooks.com

PB ISBN: 9781786829405
E ISBN: 9781786829399

Cover image courtesy of Jermyn Street Theatre

10 9 8 7 6 5 4 3 2 1

The Ice Cream Boys premiered at Jermyn Street Theatre, London on 9 October 2019 with the following cast:

JACOB ZUMA	Andrew Francis
RONNIE KASRILS	Jack Klaff
THANDI DUBE	Bu Kunene

Director	Vik Sivalingam
Set & Costume Designer	Cecilia Trono
Lighting Designer	Tim Mascall
Sound Designer	Nicola Chang
Stage Manager	Anna Short
Production Photographer	Robert Workman

Produced and general managed by Jermyn Street Theatre in association with Jeffrey T. Apter.

This play script was correct at the time of publication
but may have changed during rehearsal

Characters

RONNIE KASRILS 80
JACOB ZUMA 77
THANDI DUBE 24

The convention in this play is that THANDI plays a host of other characters that come on stage for little portfolio pieces. They always remain in one area of the stage and do not bleed into the space that is held by ZUMA and KASRILS, though there may be interactions and reactions from one area to the other.

Other characters:

ELEANOR
KATE
CHRISTIAN MISSIONARY
MEMBER OF PARLIAMENT
NELSON MANDELA
UNCLE

The setting is an expensive hospital. The stage is set in an area between private patients' rooms. There is tea and coffee in the room and chairs for patients or visitors to sit on. There are some games and newspapers including a game of chess that has been set out.

ZUMA enters from his room which is off-stage. He is angry.

ZUMA: Caw, caw. Anybody home?

Where is everybody!

Hello! Nurse! Anyone!

NURSE enters quickly.

THANDI: Mr Zuma, Mr President, hello, I'm Thandi Dube, I'm your nurse, well one of them. Not your main nurse, but I've been also assigned to you

ZUMA: Good. Well I want to

THANDI: and just one other.

ZUMA: One other? What one other?

THANDI: One other patient.

ZUMA: Which one?

THANDI: The patient opposite you.

ZUMA: Kasrils!

THANDI: Yes. You see it's efficient because I can just go from one to

ZUMA: That is the problem.

THANDI: Sorry, what's the

ZUMA: Him. Opposite me.

THANDI: But he's, it's a private room, he's not really

ZUMA: I can still see him. What I want is for you to do me a little favour.

THANDI: A favour?

ZUMA: Yes, move Mr Kasrils into another room.

THANDI: But

ZUMA: No But. Just find a room further away, far away from here, from me. And move him.

THANDI: But Mr Zuma sir, I can't do that.

ZUMA: For me, your President, you can't do something little like that?

THANDI: But there is nowhere else, Mr. President. All the rooms are full.

ZUMA: Then I must move!

THANDI: But there is nowhere. If I could...honestly.

ZUMA: There is never nowhere. There is never nohow.

THANDI: But

ZUMA: Everything is possible. Where there's a will, there's a way. I'm sure you learnt that at your mother's knee.

THANDI: Every room is full. Tomorrow. You'll be able to move tomorrow.

ZUMA: Tomorrow is no good. It must be today. Now!

THANDI: I'm so sorry, sir.

ZUMA: My daughter, let me explain. If you were in your bed, and you saw a black mamba crawling around the floor, would you turn over and go to sleep

THANDI: Ha, ha, Mr

ZUMA: or would you kill it?

THANDI: But... Mr Kasrils

ZUMA: A snake, Thandi. A vicious, dangerous snake. And what's worse, he is a snake with a smile.

THANDI: No.

ZUMA: Yes, you think, he can't be a bad man,

THANDI: He's a very nice

ZUMA: smiling with his big wide smile. But as he smiles, he grabs you, and squeezes you, and strangles you, and kills you without batting an eyelid.

THANDI: I can't believe that, sir.

ZUMA: He's a very dangerous man, Thandi.

THANDI: Surely not.

ZUMA: Do not underestimate him. Remember, he was the Minister of Intelligence, that means the nation's spymaster. A Chief of Spies is not a nice man. The people he dealt with? Spies and agents. The lowest of the low. The most vicious. The ones who would kill you as much as look at you.

THANDI: But he seems so

ZUMA: That sort do. They learn to be charming. They practise till they can twist anybody round their fingers. Especially innocent young Zulu women. Beware! Dr No, Goldfinger, Blofeld. They have nothing on him. Remember, I've known him for a very long time.

KASRILS enters finishing the last bit of an ice cream lolly.

KASRILS: Is this man letting you in on his aliases, Nurse Thandi?

THANDI: No, no, I don't think

KASRILS: Giving you a hard time?

THANDI: Thank you, Mr Kasrils. I must just

She exits.

ZUMA: Have you got something you want to say to me at long last, Kumalo?

KASRILS: Not what you want to hear, Baba.

Pause.

ZUMA: Why did my bodyguards not notice you right opposite me.

KASRILS: Maybe I was taking the sun on the balcony at the time. Your goons are slipping, aren't they, Baba.

ZUMA: Perhaps you were hiding, Kumalo.

KASRILS: I don't need to hide from you.

ZUMA: Maybe you were hiding because you know what my people do to traitors.

KASRILS: You mean, to those who stand in your way.

Pause.

ZUMA: Heh, heh, heh.

KASRILS: Ha, ha, ha.

ZUMA: Do you know what? It's actually good to see you again.

KASRILS: It seems we're neighbours again.

ZUMA: Yah!

KASRILS: But less fancy this time. No mansion in the government estate.

ZUMA: Tell me Kumalo, has the leopard changed his spots?

KASRILS: What leopard's that, Baba?

ZUMA: Well, what's a good communist like you doing in a private hospital.

KASRILS: It's my medical aid scheme. Automatic for retired ministers, as you well know. I don't see you in a state hospital.

ZUMA: Heh, heh. But I'm not claiming to be a good communist.

KASRILS: So why this one? There are others that would be far more in your league. This one isn't quite your style, a tad beneath you, I'd say.

ZUMA: Convenience.

KASRILS: What were you complaining about?

ZUMA: I wasn't complaining.

KASRILS: You said something about moving.

ZUMA: No. I'm fine.

KASRILS: Are you fine?

ZUMA: Fine, fine.

KASRILS: So why are you here?

ZUMA: I'll be fine. What about you?

KASRILS: I'm OK.

ZUMA: You're looking fat, mafuta. It's all those ice-creams.

KASRILS: I'm eighty, Jacob. I'm allowed to look fat-ish.

ZUMA: You must be careful. You'll get diabetes. Be like me, I cut out all my sugar.

KASRILS: Durban sand! White like sugar. You used to have five spoons in your tea!

ZUMA: Heh, heh.

KASRILS: No more ice-cream then?

ZUMA: Well, one has to live, ne?

KASRILS: You're looking old, Baba.

ZUMA: No, not me!

KASRILS: All the stress, huh?

ZUMA: Stress! That's a white man's problem.

KASRILS: Well, you look as though you've passed your sell-by date.

ZUMA: No, Ndoda, this spear hasn't got rusty yet.

KASRILS: Maybe it's time to put the spear down, hey Baba. Take a rest. From everything.

ZUMA: Haven't you heard, with spears, if you don't use it you lose it. Heh, heh!

Anyway, what's the matter with you, Ronnie? Why are you here?

KASRILS: Agh! Tests. They want to do tests.

ZUMA: Where?

KASRILS: My skin.

ZUMA: Your skin? What is it?

KASRILS: Possible melanoma. All that time in the sun. I'm sure it's benign.

ZUMA: Hau! That's a worry, Ronnie.

KASRILS: I'm eighty, Jacob. There's more things to worry about in this country than me having cancer. They're looking at my ankle as well.

ZUMA: The same ankle?

KASRILS: Ja, it's never been right.

ZUMA: I heard of a man with chronic pain in his ankle that turned out to be cancer.

KASRILS: Nice! What about you? What's your problem? Is it your brain?

ZUMA: My brain's in perfect working order.

KASRILS: So what is it?

ZUMA: Well

KASRILS: Go on!

ZUMA: I can't pass water. Well I can but it takes, a while. Prostate.

KASRILS: Also cancer?

ZUMA: I'm sure not.

KASRILS: There can be complications with prostate.

ZUMA: I know.

KASRILS: Impotence. In some people.

ZUMA: Aikona! Not me! No no no no. Not me.

KASRILS: Maybe it's saying, give me a break, let me have a rest!

ZUMA: Heh, heh, heh.

KASRILS: Every time I open the paper I read about another Zuma baby.

ZUMA: Heh, heh.

KASRILS: Non bloody stop.

ZUMA: It's the mark of a great man!

KASRILS: Well you made your mark alright. Twenty-two marks, hey.

ZUMA: Twenty-two, thirty-five. I'm fertile, man!

KASRILS: Well maybe that impotence is going to save the world from a thirty-sixth little Zuma.

ZUMA: Hau, Ronnie!

KASRILS: Only joking, Baba. And the current wife tally?

ZUMA: They come and go.

KASRILS: So, how many?

ZUMA: Four.

KASRILS: Ah. Plus x number of mistresses.

ZUMA: But mistresses, you see. Not girlfriends. It's a very different thing.

KASRILS: Is it?

ZUMA: Yebo! Of course. A girlfriend is temporary, will never be the wife. But with a mistress...

KASRILS: You like them young, hey Jacob.

ZUMA: And why not? Who would choose an old hen when you can have a young chick.

KASRILS: They get you into trouble.

ZUMA: Heh, heh, heh.

KASRILS: The daughter of your business acquaintance who suddenly found he was a grandfather.

ZUMA: It's good to be a grandfather.

KASRILS: But perhaps not when your grandchild's father is older than you.

ZUMA: You can't have everything. Listen. How many mistresses do some big men have? But they hide them. They have a child but they are called 'love child' and must be hidden away, frightened that one day the media will discover them. Everyone knows I love women and I love making babies.

KASRILS: The populist with the roving eye.

ZUMA: You sound jealous, Ronnie.

KASRILS: I'm not jealous of you, Baba.

ZUMA: Heh heh. You're jealous, Mfowetu.

KASRILS: Mfowetu? Your brother?

ZUMA: We will always be brothers, Ronnie.

KASRILS: Brotherhood can be a flimsy concept.

ZUMA: Or the most robust.

KASRILS: It needs love to underpin it.

ZUMA: Not every brother loves their brother or gets on with them. Some even want to kill them. Cain and Abel, heh heh.

KASRILS: I don't want to kill you.

ZUMA: Ahh, maybe not now when you see me like this. Poor Jacob unable to piss and people accusing him, maligning

9

him, turning against him. Threatened court cases, inquiries I go to out of the goodness of my heart, to help, to advise and they ask me questions, questions. I can't remember I say. How can I know all those details they ask of me?

KASRILS: They call you, Mr. I-can't-remember.

ZUMA: People laugh, they scoff. They mock me.

KASRILS: Easy to say I can't remember.

ZUMA: How can I remember everything?

KASRILS: How can you forget everything?

ZUMA: People accuse me. They have grievances, forgotten grievances, but they're quick to resurrect when weakness is *(Sniffs the air.)*

KASRILS: People are people.

ZUMA: They forget those grievances when they are against a powerful president. But once the power passes, and all that is left is a naked man, and a naked man can't hide his weak points, then the grievances resurrect with the power of a volcano. But what they don't realise is that this man here still has great power.

KASRILS: You think you're still powerful?

We hear crowds call 'ZUMA, ZUMA!'

ZUMA: Is that not power?

KASRILS: Beware the fleeting power of loyalty. It moves with a facile ease onto another.

ZUMA: Anyway, power isn't only in the position you hold. I have many children and many wives. Our ancestors are dismissive of the title President, but children, descendants, DNA, stock. They smile as the line continues like a great big railway track crossing the nation. You're just a little siding, a little narrow-gauge railway that travels up and down a minor hill.

THANDI enters.

THANDI: I need to take your blood pressure, Mr President. Would you like to follow me into your room?

ZUMA: I've got nothing to hide from him. He's seen everything.

She starts taking ZUMA's blood pressure.

KASRILS: You know I have offspring. Not thirty-five but

ZUMA: Two. I know.

THANDI: You have children, Mr Kasrils? How nice. It's good to have children. They must look after their father.

KASRILS: They're good boys. Men now of course.

THANDI: Mr Kasrils, your little procedure is booked in now for tomorrow at 10.30. Dr Kumar said he looks forward to seeing you at about 10.

KASRILS: OK.

THANDI: Please relax for me. Mr President.

ZUMA: Thandi, I am no longer President.

THANDI: A President is always a President, Mr Zuma.

ZUMA: *(Laughs genially.)* Ahhh. You see that, Ronnie! You're a good girl. Beautiful Zulu woman. Like your name, Thandi. How old are you, my daughter?

THANDI: I'm twenty-four, Mr Zuma.

ZUMA: Are you married yet? A boyfriend?

THANDI: I'm not married but I have a boyfriend, Mr Zuma.

ZUMA: You make sure he looks after you, you hear. If not, you tell him he will have me to answer to.

THANDI: He's a good man. Thank you, Mr Zuma.

ZUMA: He's a Zulu man, of course.

THANDI: Well…

ZUMA: He's not Zulu?

THANDI: He's a wonderful man.

ZUMA: What is he? Xhosa? Sotho?

THANDI: He's from Cameroon, Mr Zuma.

ZUMA: Hai! A foreigner! But you are already twenty-four. You must find a good Zulu man to marry. You can't play around much longer you know. Zulu women must marry Zulu men.

THANDI: Your blood pressure is high, sir.

I think it would be good for you to lie down for a bit. Stay calm.

ZUMA: Don't worry about me. It's been a long time since I sat down with my old comrade. You know we call him Kumalo. It's a clan name we gave him.

THANDI writes down the results in a little pad she has in her pocket.

THANDI: That's an honour for you, Mr Kasrils. I'll be back soon.

She exits.

KASRILS: So you're still President to some, I see.

ZUMA: Heh, heh.

KASRILS: After everything, huh?

ZUMA: Wherever I go, there are crowds, dancing, whistling, singing, toyi-toyiing. They call for me to be President again.

KASRILS: They don't care what you've done.

ZUMA: Hau! What have I done?

KASRILS shakes his head in disgust.

ZUMA: Nothing. I've done nothing. It's all a conspiracy. And spies.

KASRILS: Conspiracies and spies! Jislike!

ZUMA: Don't mock me, Ronnie. I know about the spies.

KASRILS: You talk kak, Jacob!

ZUMA: The ANC is full of spies and I will reveal it.

KASRILS: You point your finger at good people and denounce them as spies. But their only crime is that they've opposed you.

ZUMA: Good people? I've survived ten attempts to kill me by these same good people. I'm a dangerous person to them.

KASRILS: You're history, Jacob.

ZUMA: They thought I would disappear, but they see I haven't. So they try and poison me.

KASRILS: You're seriously paranoid, my friend.

ZUMA: That doesn't mean to say I'm wrong.

KASRILS: You're prepared to destroy the ANC to save yourself!

ZUMA: Says the man who campaigned against us!

Pause.

ZUMA: Listen, I was sorry to hear Eleanor passed on. How many years is it now? One? Two? Ten?

KASRILS is silent.

ZUMA: I passed on my condolences at the time.

KASRILS: 'A woman of principle who demonstrated great bravery resourcefulness and initiative, resolute to the people of South Africa and to the cause of freedom everywhere.'

ZUMA: You remember!

KASRILS: I was touched.

ZUMA: You didn't tell me.

KASRILS: Well 2009 wasn't exactly a good time between us.

ZUMA: Yebo, I'll never forget your treachery, but

KASRILS: Jacob! Don't exaggerate like a bloody fool. It was just plain opposition to you. Nothing to do with treachery.

ZUMA: Many have been treacherous, but yours, yours was like… Et tu, Brute.

KASRILS: Jesus! Treacherous, bloody Christ!

ZUMA: Leave it, Ronnie. I'm talking of Eleanor now.

She was quite a hero, the way she escaped from prison.

KASRILS: Brutus!

ZUMA: A white woman who escaped prison. She was, extraordinary.

KASRILS: She was.

ZUMA: Our women understood suffering.

KASRILS: Some women suffered, suffer, needlessly

ZUMA: No, no. Our comrades suffered.

KASRILS: and not just at the hands of the enemy.

ZUMA: Of course, Eleanor was lucky to be able to choose whether to suffer or not. As a privileged white woman.

KASRILS: She didn't choose to suffer, Jacob. She chose to stand up and be counted. She chose to do what was right for the people. It was a moral choice that she had to make even though she knew the terrible costs involved.

ELEANOR walks on dressed in 1960s clothes.

ELEANOR: Let me just absorb you, the sight of you. How much of you can soak into me? Will it suffice, I wonder, to last me, till I see you again. It might be years. I have no idea. I sit here watching you while you sleep and I have no idea what tomorrow will bring. Escape sounds so complete. It means it's happened, I've done it, I've got away. And maybe I will get over the border, I will make it through Botswana without being grabbed and forced back. I will get on a plane and it will fly Ronnie and me to a safe African country. Or maybe I'll be caught even before I put on my disguise and start to drive. Maybe any minute now big, vile policemen will force their way into this house and grab me and take me back to prison. And this time they'll not let me get away with escaping. This time they'll make sure I'll pay for the humiliation this white woman caused them.

You'll wake tomorrow and you'll say, where is my Mommy, and they'll answer, your Mommy has gone away. And you won't think much of it because your Mommy is often away. And from time to time you'll say, when is my Mommy coming home. And they won't answer because there is no answer and after a while you

15

won't ask anymore and a little later still you won't even think of me. I will have gone out of your life and someone else will take my place.

Please don't forget me. You must remember me. You have a mommy, one who loves you and adores you and will love you as long as she lives, whether it's in freedom or in prison.

She leaves.

KASRILS: She chose to try and help the people,

ZUMA: Look, you're actually a lucky bugger.

KASRILS: right the wrong. Fight injustice.

ZUMA: You had a good long marriage. Forty years?

KASRILS: Forty-five.

ZUMA: You see. Of course I started much later than you. Robben Island and so on.

KASRILS: You made up for it.

ZUMA: But you, we're talking about you now, you and Eleanor, it was good. I think you were a good husband, ne?

KASRILS: I always loved her, you know that, but, you know what it was like. She was left alone so much. I was hardly ever at home with her, when we lived in England and I was always

ZUMA: Being a freedom fighter.

KASRILS: The struggle.

ZUMA: Anyway, women have their children.

KASRILS: That's not always enough.

ZUMA: With reason, hey Ndoda!

KASRILS: I wanted to be with the children too.

ZUMA: Ha, Ronnie. You're actually not so different to me.
You were once also a migrant worker, like me. Back and
forth between Africa, and wife in London. You've had
three wives. So, I've had four, five.

KASRILS: Not at the same time, Jacob.

ZUMA: So what? Your timing was just a bit different to mine.
You loved them all though.

KASRILS: I didn't give any of mine 'twenty-four years of hell'.

ZUMA pauses, shocked.

ZUMA: Ah, look, there's a chess set. How about a game, huh,
like old times?

KASRILS: Twenty-four years of hell.

ZUMA setting up chess board says nothing.

KASRILS: How did you feel when you heard she'd left a note?

ZUMA: White. I go first!

KASRILS: A note saying she'd had, twenty-four

ZUMA: Are you going to say it again?

KASRILS: years of hell.

ZUMA says nothing.

KASRILS: I liked Kate. I remember the first time I met her.
Do you remember Jacob, we were in a car in Maputo,
driving through the streets. A few days to relax before we
returned to the training camps. A few days to feel young,
free and alive. You stopped to pick up a pretty young
woman.

KATE walks in.

KASRILS: You introduced me to her.

KATE: Pleased to meet you.

ZUMA: You're playing games, Ndoda. U'ya dladla. You are trying to make me feel guilty.

KASRILS: Should you be feeling guilty, Mfowetu?

ZUMA: I don't have time to feel guilt, or remorse. Ten years in jail, fifteen years in exile. I had to catch up on living.

KASRILS: At someone else's expense.

ZUMA: It's easy at the end to say twenty-four years of hell.

(To KATE.) Why didn't you go

KATE: I was lying on a bed of needles.

ZUMA: at any time during those twenty-four years?

KATE: When you crawl so long and your knees are bleeding, you fear to stand.

ZUMA: *(To KATE.)* Why would anyone live through twenty-four years of hell without doing something about it?

KATE: I could see many doors in but no door out.

ZUMA: What does it make you? Pathetic or a victim? You could have left.

KATE: I couldn't find my path. The way out was too dark. I couldn't see where to step my feet.

ZUMA: *(To KASRILS.)* One had already divorced me. There was a precedent.

(To KATE.) You left your children behind!

KATE: I couldn't take them where I had to go.

ZUMA: *(To KATE.)* You didn't have to go anywhere!

(To KASRILS.) I can tell you, she was a very difficult woman.

KASRILS: Meaning?

ZUMA: Well, you know she left a farewell note.

KASRILS: You mean a suicide note.

ZUMA: You and your Mbeki men concealed it and then leaked it to the Press when it would do me the most damage.

KASRILS: Ha, another conspiracy!

ZUMA: You wanted to use it as propaganda.

KASRILS: Always someone else is to blame.

KATE: I wish you success with new Makoti and would advise her that the seat she is going to occupy is very, very, very Hot.

KASRILS: Capital H. What did she mean by that?

ZUMA: *(To KATE.)* Exactly! What did you mean by that?

KATE: What do you think?

ZUMA: *(To KATE.)* Did you want me just for yourself?

KATE: Your touch made me feel as if I had been walking through heavy rain while carrying a basket on my head full of the hottest bonnet peppers.

KASRILS: Ughhh. Painful. Maybe she wanted more from you.

ZUMA: *(To KATE.)* Maluka! Crazy in the kop! Impossible to have near me. You never understood me.

(To KASRILS.) These Mozambican women, shuuu. They are, very difficult.

(To KATE.) Eich, to go and kill yourself!

KATE exits.

(To KASRILS.) Why do you bring this up?

KASRILS: You make women suffer.

ZUMA: Me? I care for women. I want to pleasure them.

KASRILS: You cause misery everywhere you go.

ZUMA: Did I keep her locked in a room? Did I make a slave of her? No! She was treated like a queen. I love women. Women. Not one woman. Take it or leave me.

ZUMA toys with the chess pieces.

KASRILS: Come on, let's play.

They start to play.

KASRILS: Hmm, queen's pawn opener. Using your lady to sacrifice a pawn. Ha!

ZUMA: And your old Maputo defence, yah! that deceptive move to divert your opponent's attention. Heh! I'll get you.

They play for a while.

KASRILS: Ja, it must be hard for you to satisfy so many women at once.

ZUMA: It's not hard for me, Ronnie. That is the skill I possess.

KASRILS: A big man like you.

ZUMA: You're being sarcastic, Ronnie. You know our Zulu culture is polygamous.

KASRILS: You just want to compete with your King and his seven wives and god knows how many children.

ZUMA: Wait, can you smell that rancid, burning, sour smell? Do you recognise it? Maybe you're a little too close to it. Maybe you've never smelt it from this side. I know it well. It's called 'white man' attitude.

KASRILS: It's not me who has something to prove.

ZUMA: That the white man's way is the right way. I see you still have colonial blood running through your veins.

KASRILS: Born and bred in Jo'burg. A product of the struggle.

ZUMA: But white. You grew up when South Africa was still a British colony. Queen Elizabeth was your queen. Did you love your queen when you were a little boy, Ronnie? Did you wish one day you'd go and have tea with the Queen?

KASRILS: Watch your queen! *(Moves a piece.)* Jewish, Jacob. Hardly applied.

ZUMA: You Jewish! MaJuta. You're very far removed from your tribe. MaJuta. You never even married a Jewish woman! Irish, Scottish, and now Muslim. Why no Jewess? You're a very strange Jew. A Jew who isn't interested in making imali. I don't trust such men. You prefer mischief to money, Ndoda.

KASRILS: Not all Jews want money.

ZUMA: *(Moves a piece.)* Here comes my sainted bishop. You're more Christian than Jewish, like those Christian missionaries who tried to change our traditional ways?

Enter CHRISTIAN MISSIONARY.

CM: Oh no no no. You cannot have more than one wife. It is entirely against the Bible's teaching.

ZUMA: *(To KASRILS.)* They forget so conveniently that Solomon and David had wives and concubines.

CM: You must emulate us, our western civilisation. It is the highest moral code.

ZUMA: You trample over traditions and traditional ways that have formed the structure of our society, that worked for hundreds of years.

CM: We bring light into the darkness.

ZUMA: You think you know what is best for others. You told us we needed to wear clothes. So traders came to sell us clothes. And then of course the soldiers came to protect the traders and their property.

CM: We brought education, health, enlightenment. We provided orphanages and old-aged homes.

ZUMA: That's it Ronnie, look at that! That's my point exactly! There were no orphans. The people took them into their homes and they became part of their families. The elderly were cared for, they were venerated. *(To CM.)* You found a solution, but to a problem you created yourselves!

CM: We provide missionary hospitals.

ZUMA: But you introduced the killer diseases into the original populations?

CM: We are not exclusively to blame. Traders were responsible too.

ZUMA: You supported slavery.

CM: We fought vociferously against slavery. We showed how the problems that were created were because the Boers and the British threw the people off their lands.

ZUMA: You were able to do what you did, behave as you did, because you didn't see the people in South Africa as people. To you, we were closer to animals. Sub-humans.

CM: What can I say?

CM exits.

KASRILS: Respect, lack of respect, it's so basic to the problem and the solution.

ZUMA: You only know respect. What do you know about disrespect?

KASRILS: Are you kidding me? It's not enough that I am a communist. I am an anti-Zionist Jew. I know disrespect every day of my life from those who can't tolerate my ideology.

ZUMA: We're not that different Ronnie. We were once joined at the hip. We did the same things. We took the same risks. We ate the same food, we ran, we fought, we cried over the same comrades who were killed. We looked out for each other. We looked after each other. For years we slept next to each other. We sang the same songs.

He starts singing quietly hamba Kahle uMkhontowe'm Khonto uMkhonto weSizwe https://www.youtube.com/ watch?v=-lFhEfKurjU

ZUMA: We were strong together.

KASRILS: We were.

ZUMA: We could do anything together.

KASRILS: Anything. We were going to change the world.

ZUMA: Make it a better place.

KASRILS: No white, no black, no rich, no poor.

ZUMA: We could have carried on making a difference, Ronnie.

KASRILS: I agree.

ZUMA: We could have been a force to be reckoned with.

KASRILS: Yes!

ZUMA: You know… we still can!

KASRILS: That time is long past, Msholozi.

KASRILS sings again and after a few moments ZUMA joins in. THANDI comes in and joins the singing. After it is over, they laugh and she hands ZUMA some pills which he swallows with water.

ZUMA: You know our songs, Thandi, even though it was from long before you were born.

THANDI: I used to sing them with my mother.

They continue with the chess.

ZUMA: Ha! Knight takes pawn.

KASRILS: I wonder if Nurse Thandi knows what your middle name is, Msholozi.

THANDI: Oh, you use Mr Zuma's clan name. That is nice.

ZUMA: Of course she knows. They all know. Come on, in your best Zulu accent.

KASRILS: Check. Gedleyilekisa.

ZUMA: Shuww. Very good.

THANDI: Hau, Mr Kasrils, you speak Zulu well. He spoke to me in Zulu when he first came in, you know.

ZUMA: Really? And how long did it last?

THANDI: Just good morning, how are you.

ZUMA: Then?

THANDI: English!

ZUMA: *(In Zulu.) What can you expect from these whites. They live here all their lives and never learn to speak our language.)* Yini ongayilindela kulaba bakoloni abamhlophe. Bahlala lapha konke ukuphila kwabo futhi abakaze bafunde ukukhuluma ulimi lwethu

THANDI: *(Laughing, but embarrassed.)* Hau, Mr Zuma Sir! I was brought up in a household where the talk was of the struggle years with praise for those who fought. Madiba, of course, Mr Sisulu, Mr Zuma, many more. And there were some whites too who were loved. Mr Slovo, Mr Kasrils, Mrs First

ZUMA: You know, Ronnie, even some of the Boers can speak our languages. Check.

KASRILS: Yes, but only for purposes of power and control. A very silly move, Baba. You must be slipping. So Nurse, tell me, what does his name mean.

THANDI: Gedleyilekisa. He who stabs you in the back while smiling.

ZUMA: Heh heh!

KASRILS: Heh heh?

ZUMA: Heh heh!

KASRILS: Do you want to hear a story, Nurse? It's a story of a much younger Mr Zuma and me.

THANDI: Yes, of course I do. I know he was a big freedom fighter. But you were too, Mr Kasrils.

KASRILS: Well this is a story of just the two of us. One night, Mr Zuma and I were in Mozambique and we were crossing over the border illegally to Swaziland. We had big backpacks, heavy, full of ammunition which we were taking over to our comrades. We set off. It was a good night because it was bad weather, and bad weather should keep the enemy away. We even laughed and joked. Remember, Baba?

ZUMA: There were many such nights.

KASRILS: But you'll remember this night. Just the weather for violating the frontier, eh Baba.

ZUMA: Yebo, Homeboy. Like amaRussia used to say; bad weather is the guerilla's best friend.

KASRILS: Let's hope the Swazi men are doing their 'thing' on a night like this, instead of sniffing around the border.

ZUMA: Some would rather be in bed with the 'blanket'.

ZUMA/KASRILS: Sniffing the blanket!

They chuckle.

KASRILS: Yes, you remember well. Unfortunately, as I jumped over the border fence, I landed on a stone, and fell and twisted my ankle very badly.

THANDI: Shu. Your bad ankle?

KASRILS: That's when it started.

ZUMA: I thought he'd broken it.

KASRILS: I tried to carry on.

ZUMA: He couldn't. I insisted we went back. I helped you, you leaned on me. We went back to Ma Isabella. She lay you down on a bed and made sure you were as comfortable as possible.

KASRILS: She did, you both did. You came and gave me coffee and went back into the kitchen. I thought to myself how lucky to have a comrade who looks out for me, who cares for me. I was half asleep, but heard you talking together 'Aii Mama, it was an important mission. All that ammunition we had to get across the border. Our comrades needed it. What can you expect of a stupid umlungu mampara!' You both laughed!

THANDI: You understood him?

KASRILS: I understood that he said *white* fool. Not a fool. Not his brother the fool, his comrade the fool, who spoilt the mission. But a *white* fool who spoilt the mission.

ZUMA: Have you looked at yourself in the mirror recently, Mampara.

KASRILS: I haven't seen white or black since I was twenty-one. To me everyone was either a comrade or an enemy. But to you, I was

ZUMA: Privileged.

KASRILS: Umlungu. White!

ZUMA: You are what you are. Even in chess white has the initial advantage.

KASRILS: That's chess. I don't see a person's colour!

ZUMA: Don't tell me you don't see black and white. We all do.

THANDI: Gentlemen. White and black, it's not important. The rainbow nation, Madiba said.

ZUMA: Do you trust a man who says he doesn't see colour? What does it even mean? You don't notice the sky is blue, the grass is green, the ice cream's white? Are you colour blind? Is that what you want us to believe?

27

KASRILS: When I look at a person, I see their face, a smile, a snarl, a handsome man, a scarred woman. When they say, please baas, give me some money. Then I see that it's a black man. I see it because I need to know if it's still always the black people that are begging for money.

THANDI: I see white men begging too.

KASRILS: Yes, and how surprised and horrified are we when we see white men begging. Broken whites with dirty signs. Hungry. Help me. Homeless. But when we see black men, black women, old blind black women, ancient decrepit black men, tiny children all begging, wearing rags, no shoes in winter, sleeping on the streets. Why aren't we shocked by that? Why is it so acceptable because they're black? Because it's been happening for years and we are so damn used to it!

ZUMA: We are the product of the struggle against apartheid and colonialism. Such struggles don't leave you when they are won. They change your essence, your DNA. You become a misaligned person, someone who has lost his ground. So we twist and we turn inside ourselves until we find some way of being able to stand up straight and see who we are. Until we find an identity that matches what we feel.

KASRILS: Agh, shame Jacob! Unable to find yourself. Maybe you need some counselling, Mfowetu. Some mindfulness workshops.

ZUMA: After all these years of being in the struggle, of being such a big man in the struggle with your AK47, your commitment and your sacrifices, your spies, you haven't even grasped the basics of it all yet.

KASRILS: I know South Africa. I know what it's all about.

ZUMA: You know it. But you don't know it.

KASRILS: I know it was different for you and me. I'm not such a, mampara. Samora and Cabral, and Luthuli, they all said the tribe must die for the nation to be born. South Africa belongs to all who live in it.

ZUMA: You know why you don't know? Because it wasn't you. You didn't live it. Oh yes, 'I can imagine how you felt. I can feel for you, my brother'. No. You can't. You can never. Because you are white and it never happened to you.

THANDI: Apartheid was over before I was born. I never knew really what it was like. For me it's, stories.

ZUMA: Yebo, I'm sure you've heard the story of the boy who looked after the herd of goats, not even cows, just goats, who lived with his grandparents, too poor to send him to school, who tried to teach himself to read while his friends laughed at him. 'Heh heh, look at that poor goatherd, not even cows, just goats.' Whose mother lived far away from him, working as a domestic servant for a white family. She was a 'girl', a 'maid'. If he wanted to see his mother, he had to go to where she lived and hide, because she couldn't have her children stay with her, in a white area, with her white madam and white baas. Perhaps you can't imagine the humiliation the boy felt, not only for her but for him too, when he heard the way they spoke to her, get this, do that. The way she spoke to them, yes please madam, no thank you baas.

THANDI: I know many women who still work for white people and call them madam and baas. Of course, I am a black nurse looking after a black and white man. That would never have happened before, isn't it?

ZUMA: It's very different now. We made it different for you. We went through the struggles so your generation doesn't have to.

THANDI: Now we can live where we want to.

KASRILS: Where do you live?

THANDI: Alexandra Township.

KASRILS: Why not Sandton? Why shouldn't you live in a rich suburb?

THANDI: The only place I would be able to live in Sandton is in a rich family's servants' quarters. But, I am a few steps above that. So I can live in my own shack in Alex, and know that as long as it doesn't rain there won't be mud. And in three more years, I'll have enough money to buy a house made of bricks with a toilet indoors so I don't have to use a bucket because I might get attacked if I go outside at night.

KASRILS: What work does your boyfriend do, Nurse Thandi?

THANDI: He doesn't have a job at the moment.

THANDI exits. They continue to play chess.

KASRILS: Is that black and white, Jacob, or is it Marx's class struggle?

ZUMA: Racism crosses class boundaries Ronnie. When we have equal proportions of black and white poor, black and white unemployed, we'll discuss Marx, OK?

KASRILS: You've just lost your castle.

ZUMA: I've got a second one.

KASRILS: I'm not talking about your Nkandla.

ZUMA: Nkandla? Nkaaandla! Heh heh, you sound just like those whites at Question Time in Parliament.

MP walks in.

MP: Mr President, can you explain to the House how millions of Rand in wasteful and unauthorised expenditure on Nkaaanndla was allowed,

ZUMA: Nkaaanndla!!

MP: when we have a crisis in this country resulting in no school books, insufficient educational opportunities, lack of medicine and medical care, housing that is a disgrace for a country where the President allows himself to take 246 million rand

ZUMA: For security!

MP: of public money

ZUMA: I paid it back.

MP: for his homestead Nkaaandla.

ZUMA: Nkaaandla! Heh heh.

KASRILS: Out of 246 million, you paid back 7.8.

MP: And where did that money come from?

ZUMA: Go away, you. Shuuu!

MP exits.

KASRILS: My brother in the bush would never have used public money to improve his homestead!

ZUMA: Your brother in the bush had nothing.

KASRILS: He had morality. Revolutionary morality.

ZUMA: People change. They move on. Grow up.

KASRILS: Become morally corrupt.

ZUMA: You might have your morality. But it's not revolutionary morality.

KASRILS: What is it?

ZUMA: Bourgeois morality.

KASRILS: Ha!

ZUMA: Yes, the morality that comes easily when you sit with no fear, no hunger, or thirst, or desperation. It's easy then to know what everyone should do and how everyone should behave.

KASRILS: You sold whatever was left of your morality to the highest bidder. And now you're an, empty vessel. Making the loudest noise.

ZUMA: Do you know who said that?

KASRILS: Shakespeare?

ZUMA: Ha! Plato! Heh, heh. I got you there, Mfowetu!

KASRILS: *(Laughs.)* Hai, Baba. It breaks my heart when I see where you've come from and what you are now.

ZUMA: I deserve a better life than I had, Kumalo!

KASRILS: Yes, you do. But so do others. Many don't have a better life.

ZUMA: We suffered for it, for the struggle.

KASRILS: Many suffered.

ZUMA: You can't compare us with those people who just

KASRILS: Just what?

ZUMA: Just lived. Were passive.

KASRILS: They might not have had guns in their hands, but they lived the struggle every day, year upon year, with their passes, their hostels, their poverty, the violence they had to endure every single day of their lives.

ZUMA: You can't compare that with what we went through. What we gave up. My ten years on Robben Island. Twenty-one years old to thirty-one. My twenties. Stuck at the quarry breaking rocks into stones, blisters, bloodied hands, aching muscles. Sleeping on cold cement floors, winter, summer, three blankets and a thin sisal mat. Cold showers for ten years. And the delightful tausa ritual. You know what that is, don't you Ronnie.

KASRILS: I know.

VOICE OVER *(Prison Officer.)*: *Jump prisoner, star jumps, wider, wider!*

ZUMA: Naked inspection so that anything hidden up our arses, falls out.

KASRILS: I said I know.

ZUMA: Easier for them than having to stick their fingers up our black arses.

KASRILS: Jesus Jacob!

ZUMA *(As PO.)*: You, kaffir, stop talking, knees up run, hup, hup, hup.

ZUMA: I had no visitors. Not one person in ten years.

KASRILS: You told your mother not to come.

ZUMA: She was a domestic worker in Durban. How could she come? She needed her money for her children, not to spend it all getting to Cape Town then the ferry to Robben Island for a half hour visit.

And after that, exile, training camps, combat, attack, retreat, escape by the skin of our teeth. *(Makes like a pistol with his fingers and imitates the sounds of shots.)* Etwa, etwa.

You can't compare them with us. We suffered more.

KASRILS: What are you getting at?

ZUMA: That it's our time to eat.

KASRILS: Doesn't everyone who suffered need to eat.

ZUMA: Those who suffered more, get more.

KASRILS: So some are more equal than others.

ZUMA: And why not!

KASRILS: Bloody animal farm. Baa, baa, black sheep. And you and the Guptas take all the wool!

ZUMA: They were entrepreneurs! They were my business colleagues!

KASRILS: They were your masters!

ZUMA: Be careful, mfowetu. You risk suggesting I was a slave to another master.

KASRILS: Is that so far from the truth?

ZUMA: I wanted them to have a newspaper and a television station to put my side forward. I abused them, exploited them, not the other way round.

KASRILS: The saddest thing with liars is when they lie to themselves.

ZUMA: You make serious allegations.

KASRILS: Easily proven, my brother.

ZUMA: Haii. You step on dangerous waters, my friend.

KASRILS: You are not a crocodile. I don't fear you! Your teeth are blunt. What will you do? Snap me with your gums!

Pause.

ZUMA: Ronnie, you know what your problem is?

KASRILS: I'm not the one with the problem.

ZUMA: You think you are one of us. Because you have been part of the struggle, you think that it makes you an honorary black man.

KASRILS: You mean like Japanese were honorary whites at the time of Apartheid. You're sick, man.

ZUMA: You are not a black man. You are a white mampara. There is one thing that has put you on the other side of the fence, and you can never see what it is like to be on ours.

KASRILS: And what's that?

ZUMA: Privilege. There's us and there's you, and the dividing line is privilege, because privilege does something to the brain. It makes it essentially different. As a child you had people around you who loved you, and had time to love you, and hold you, and give you whatever you needed.

You never knew the fear that could grip with such terror when the sirens of police cars got nearer and stopped, right there, and you heard the paap, paap, paap of the guns thudding next to you. Your brain's synapses were able to make connections and develop in strength while ours struggled through deprivation and loss and fear and emptiness.

KASRILS: There are people born privileged who may have a strong sense of morality, justice, kindness, goodness, loyalty, fairness. All of these things affect how people behave. If what you say is true, the non-privileged would have all the excuses in the world to behave as you have. No wonder you think you could get away with anything. You have something totally in common with the Trumps of the world, the ultra-privileged. You know what that is?

Entitlement.

You think you deserve and should get everything because once you had nothing.

ZUMA: And you know you deserve and should get everything because that is the way it's always been. And you know that for you elitists, that's the way it's going to carry on.

Why shouldn't I be part of your elite club, hey? Why should I not have what whites have?

KASRILS: I'm not talking about not having. It's the level of magnitude I'm talking about.

ZUMA: When I got home from exile, what did I have? Nothing. No property, no bank account, no savings. Nothing. But I had three wives at that time, children to house, to feed, to educate, to look after.

KASRILS: So of course that meant you could accept 'well-wishers'

From the wings we see a hand in view offering bundles of cash, another with an expensive shirt.

KASRILS: buying you fancy shirts, filling your car with petrol, even paying for the car wash! Didn't you ever ask yourself where it would lead to?

ZUMA: Those white millionaires, billionaires. The whites who continue to have, and continue to have, and continue to have. They had it all the way through the apartheid years and now, after everything we've been through, they continue to have.

KASRILS: So you want to be one of those three men who have as much wealth as half the 56 million in this country?

ZUMA: Three *white* men, Ronnie!

KASRILS: Fat cat bastard capitalist shitholes. Is that what you want? Is that what you fought for, all those years, all those hardships and desperate times. So that you can be one of the richest men in the country?

ZUMA: Why should this man here not be rich? Can you tell me that? Why should those three men have it all and not this one here?

KASRILS: Because you are better than that. You were once a good communist, Jacob. What happened?

ZUMA: I grew up.

KASRILS: Don't give me that bullshit. Don't tell me that comrade, that idealist, the man who wanted a society based on principles of social justice, real equality, freedom from want...

ZUMA: Slogans, man, slogans.

KASRILS: We used to read the Communist Manifesto together on Sunday mornings in Maputo, for Christ's sake.

ZUMA: Our 'church readings'.

KASRILS: Yes! 'Time for our church readings', you'd say.

They both laugh.

KASRILS: The comrade I knew hated the fact that the propertied classes owned the land, the means of producing wealth, lording it over the majority, the state serving their interests.

ZUMA: How long has it been around, those principles, a hundred years, more? Right, tell me where they work? Anywhere? Go on, tell me. East Germany? Kaput! Soviet Union? Kaput! Putin's Russia? He's the richest man in the world. China? Vietnam? Heh heh. They love capitalism. Cuba? North Korea? You want that? Not me. Not here.

People change Ronnie. People change with the times. How many good communists are there now in South Africa, hey? You? Last man standing. You know it makes you look

KASRILS: What?

ZUMA: Pathetic. Like a mampara. Come into the 21st century, Ronnie. The water's good.

KASRILS: Ja, the water's good, the water's sweet, but for whom? You've got to think of the poor, Jacob. You can't forget them now. All those jobless, homeless, the uneducated, the hungry. We've got to continue the fight for them.

ZUMA: They are my constituents. I haven't forgotten them.

KASRILS: The ANC is, was, a pro-poor organisation. How is it possible that we could allow, bloody enable, such inequality?

ZUMA: You were part of the government, Ronnie. Are you blameless?

KASRILS: No.

ZUMA: There you are.

KASRILS: But we were getting there.

ZUMA: With Mbeki? Please!

KASRILS: You diverted it all, Jacob. You built a dam to stop the river flowing in the way it should have flowed. You diverted it and made it take an unnatural course.

ZUMA: It was long before me. When the country could have gone down the path of changing things for the poor, when Mandela came back from Davos in 1992…

MANDELA enters.

MANDELA: Ahem... Now listen, what I hear in Davos from world leaders is sobering. They view our Freedom Charter as a socialist document. The economic clauses on land and nationalisation at any rate. If we implement socialist policies we will have no foreign investment and we'll end up as a pariah state, isolated, like Cuba.

ZUMA: *(To KASRILS.)* Why aren't you arguing against him. We're all sitting back and taking it. Why? Because it's Madiba, or because we know what he's saying is true.

KASRILS: With all due respect, comrade Mandela, land redistribution and nationalisation of specific industries like iron and steel is not socialism. It's been done in capitalist countries like Sweden to good effect and Britain's welfare state after the war.

MANDELA: The world today is a vastly different place to then. Without foreign investment we will never get our economy going.

KASRILS: I beg to differ Madiba. Foreign investors will only be drawn to South Africa when we get our economy going.

MANDELA: They will only invest when we have political stability. And that means big business at home and abroad, the Oppenheimers in South Africa and the Rockefellers in America, will only support our political transition if we can guarantee economic stability. Your socialism will wreck our dream of political power. We must oppose populism and accept that now is the time for compromise.

Sound of cheering and clapping. Viva Mandela! Viva ANC!

KASRILS: Of course Madiba, we are not at a stage of socialist revolution. We have already accepted the need for compromise and negotiation. We overthrew apartheid through our collective action. The people expect more than political power. We need to be bold and have the political will to begin to transform the economy so that it serves the people and not an economic elite. We need to do that now while the people, and especially the workers, are united and strong. If we do not take decisive steps while the situation is favourable the chance will be gone.

Shouts of Amandla! Power to the people!

MANDELA exits.

ZUMA: You didn't say that.

KASRILS: No.

ZUMA: You said nothing.

KASRILS: I wish I had.

ZUMA: You could have changed everything. But you were too much of a jellyfish to challenge Madiba, the people's hero!

KASRILS: We were sleepwalking. But we could have righted it when we woke up. We would have got there. If we'd stayed true to our ideals. But it was too late. You made it too late.

ZUMA: Yebo! Always blame me. But it would never have gone the way you wanted. And you know why? Because your ANC comrades, your communist cadres, they were right there next to me taking the top posts, the best pickings, pushing people aside to get to the feeding trough. We were all entitled, no matter how strong our communist fervour. We all knew it was our turn now. Did we do so wrong?

KASRILS: What you did, Jacob, is the law of the jungle.
You diverted millions, billions that should have gone to
improving the living conditions of the

ZUMA: Bollocks! It doesn't work like that.

KASRILS: But who got it? You, and your cronies, your Guptas,
the parasites. Your wives, family business enterprises, your
mistresses. Your children.

ZUMA: Leave my children out of it.

KASRILS: Your Nkandla castle with its countless rooms, cattle
kraal, its dove cote, its amphitheatre, its *fire* pool.

ZUMA: Swimming pool! Those idiots from Public Works
called it fire pool to cover their arses.

KASRILS: Your petty favours led to arms deals for your
benefactors and for crooked tycoons. And the result, the
result is devastation,

ZUMA: You spurt like the Daily Maverick.

KASRILS: for workers, the unemployed, the marginalised,
women, youth, the aged, the economy,

ZUMA: He goes on and on

KASRILS: land, water, the environment.

ZUMA: A very nice speech. Well done. Worthy of the
communist politician who kept his hands clean. I salute
your moral superiority.

KASRILS: What would your mother say if she could see you
now!

ZUMA: She would be proud of me.

KASRILS: Proud of you? Living off the backs of people
like her.

ZUMA: Proud.

KASRILS: Thank goodness she didn't live long enough to see what you became.

ZUMA: She was always proud!

KASRILS: The last time she was proud was when you went off to become a freedom fighter.

Zuma's UNCLE walks in.

UNCLE: Lalela m'fanakiti – wena *(Listen home boy.)* You can't go running around like some tsotsi from town.

ZUMA: But I want to fight, Uncle.

UNCLE: Yah, you want to go and fight to free our people. But tell me, big one, who will feed your family when you are away?

ZUMA: I need to fight, Uncle.

UNCLE: Who will find the money for your brothers and sisters to go to school? Who will pay the rent? Yes, go think of everyone else. Forget your family. Let them struggle without you. Do you think they will smile and say, our brother is fighting for our freedom, when they sit at the table and have only water for breakfast. Wena indod Msholozi, you son of Msholozi. You stay put pakati ekaya, Inside your home!

UNCLE exits.

ZUMA: She was proud. Even when her brother berated me.

But you see, Ronnie, her pride was unsustainable. It disintegrates when you know your children are hungry.

Was I right to go? Would you have gone, or stayed and looked after your family?

KASRILS: The same as you, my brother. You were the bravest of us all. The first to respond. The first to help. The first to go. You were a lion, Jacob. And I loved that lion.

ZUMA: Ronnie, listen to me. I want to talk to you, my brother.

KASRILS: I'm listening, Mfowetu.

ZUMA: We both know that our ranks are riddled with spies from top to bottom.

KASRILS: Don't talk of spies, Jacob. You use it as a diversion from your crimes.

ZUMA: You can help me and yourself. We can do it together. Once again, we can achieve great things together!

KASRILS: What are you talking about?

ZUMA: They mock me when I say there are spies. They say, just like you, that I'm paranoid. But if you said it as well, people wouldn't mock. People wouldn't scorn. Don't you want to rid our ANC of all those izimpimpi, all those bloody spies and agents. We're both former spy chiefs, we can be a powerful combo. You and me together, Ronnie, I'm telling you. We can get back into power! Power and prominence and we'll put the country right!

Pause.

ZUMA: Don't you want your life to carry on meaning something, not just be an old man who has no position and nothing to do. Just wait to die.

KASRILS: I want to rid the ANC of corruption. Will you work with me to do that? Will you come clean, will you speak up? Will you testify? Will you do that, Jacob?

ZUMA: Why must you always muddy the water?

KASRILS: Corruption is the mud in the water. Not make-believe spies. We have to sift it out and get rid of it. If we don't, we won't have a country. Not the country we both fought for.

ZUMA: You mampara you. Of course you wouldn't come with me. What was I thinking? I was a fool to give you a chance. Why would that old-school, blinkered, better-than-thou, I've got the moral high ground, moralistic, patronising, superior Communist take a chance.

KASRILS: You know something? I agree. I do have the moral high ground, because those principles we both fought for are not relevant one day and not the next, right one day and not the next. They are fundamental principles.

THANDI enters and brings them a tray with tea.

THANDI: Some tea for you both?

ZUMA: Ahh Thandi, just in time to save me from this old man's haranguing.

THANDI: Milk?

KASRILS: Jacob, you've got to stop. Don't you care that you and your followers will take our country to the brink of civil war?

ZUMA: I will speak to my people if they ask me to!

KASRILS: It's so volatile. You're fanning the winds. It'll be another Rwanda.

ZUMA: Rwanda!

KASRILS: And for what? One goal, one aim that surpasses everything else. To engineer your own come-back. To be President again.

ZUMA: Ha!

She gives them tea.

ZUMA/KASRILS: Thank you.

THANDI: You're welcome! If you want more tea, just ring the bell.

As she exits, KASRILS notices how ZUMA stares at her backside.

KASRILS: Jesu, Baba. You're as bad as that bastard Trump. When are you going to grow up? Umtonto we Sizwe than Umkhonto we Sizwe!

ZUMA: That's good Kumalo! Penis of the nation! Clever, I like it!

He laughs.

ZUMA: But you are a hypocrite! You might not look now, but how loyal were you to Eleanor when you were in the bush? All those beautiful black comrades in Angola, Mozambique.

KASRILS: Beauty and brains, so dignified and alluring in their kangas, those beautiful sarongs.

ZUMA: Every camp commander had a 'blanket' to keep himself warm. You never turned your blanket down, did you, Kumalo? We had some times, hey!

KASRILS: I never took advantage of our recruits, everyone knows that! I slept alone.

ZUMA: What about Maputo? Swazi

KASRILS: Princesses!

ZUMA: With red feathers

KASRILS: in their hair

ZUMA: Yebo.

They bow and laugh.

ZUMA: Long live we-men! *(Laughs at his joke.)*

KASRILS: Your queen's in trouble.

He moves his piece and they play a few moves.

ZUMA: You know Kumalo. I'm not a bad man. You speak as if I'm the devil.

KASRILS: I didn't say you were but I'll never forgive you for what you did. You can try explain it away but we both know it was a terrible thing you did.

ZUMA: No, you're wrong Kumalo. You've always had that wrong. And you've never apologised.

KASRILS: I've nothing to apologise for!

ZUMA: You caused me a lot of trouble, Ronnie. Tell me now that you're sorry.

KASRILS: It's for you to say sorry to her!

ZUMA: You were wrong. I may have been mistaken. But you were wrong!

KASRILS: She phoned me.

ZUMA: You made her take it further. Look what it did to her. Who suffered? Only her!

KASRILS: I hadn't seen her in six months. She phoned me. I was disgusted, beyond anything I'd heard in my life, Jacob.

ZUMA: You did it just to get at me! But it backfired on you! You were the one who was devious, who looked a fool in the eyes of the ANC. The man who organised a honey trap.

KASRILS: Only in the eyes of your fanatic supporters. Everyone else in the country knew it was nonsense, all lies, that I had nothing to do with it. Even to this day, I hear her over and over.

THANDI enters.

THANDI: Mr Zuma! Mr Kasrils! What is the matter? What's going on here? Please, this is a hospital. We have sick patients here.

KASRILS: I still feel numb with shock. Are you sure, I said on the phone. Is there a witness? Of course there isn't. Have you been to a doctor? Is there any proof? How are you coping? Questions, questions. I put off the main question, the one I resist for as long as I could. But eventually I ask it. What do you want me to do? But I get in quickly, I speak before she can, I say, you do understand that if I get involved they'll use it against you, they'll say I set you up.

I've got to get away from him!

KASRILS exits.

THANDI: What was that all about?

ZUMA: Nothing. Don't worry your pretty little head about it.

THANDI: I am surprised you're both so rude to each other?

ZUMA: Are we? I don't think so.

THANDI: I told my mother you were both coming and I was to look after you. She was surprised. She said you were comrades but then he left the government when you took over from Mr Mbeki. My mother wondered why someone who fought for the ANC all his life would campaign against it once you had become President.

ZUMA: It's simple. You can tell her he's a traitor.

THANDI: Is he?

ZUMA: Yes. People aren't always what they seem. You must be careful, Thandi. You're an innocent, naïve. People can be, devious, not good.

THANDI: My mother says I must beware

ZUMA: That's why you need people to protect you.

THANDI: of jackals wearing sheep's clothing.

ZUMA: Exactly. She's right. And isn't a jackal a perfect description of him. You can't trust a thing he says. Pasop, my child. Beware.

You should come and visit me. I have a beautiful townhouse in Johannesburg.

THANDI: I know, I've seen it on television.

ZUMA: Wouldn't you like to see it in person? I'm sure you like gardens. I'll show you our garden. It's very beautiful.

THANDI: I'm sure it is.

ZUMA: One day, instead of going all the way back to Alex after work, you can come and stay at my house. I have many rooms. You can spend the night.

THANDI: I can get back to Alex, I don't mind travelling, Mr Zuma.

ZUMA: But the taxis, the inconvenience, the expense.

THANDI: It's not a problem for me.

ZUMA: Taxis are terrible. Dangerous. You know traffic lights for them are there just as a suggestion. You take your life in your hands.

THANDI: I'm alright.

ZUMA: Or perhaps you would like to come to Nkandla. You could bring your swimming costume and have a swim in the pool there. The air is very special in Nkandla.

THANDI: I don't go back to KwaZulu very often.

ZUMA: If you come, you will see what it is to be treated like the Queen you are.

THANDI: I'm not a queen, Mr Zuma.

ZUMA: To me you are a queen. You know you are very pretty.

THANDI doesn't answer.

ZUMA: Surely your boyfriend tells you.

She doesn't respond.

ZUMA: You see, there are advantages to being with someone, more experienced.

THANDI: I'm fine with him.

ZUMA: Of course you're not. Come, *(He moves towards her and puts his arms around her.)* let me show you how a President can kiss a queen.

He tries to kiss her. She pushes him away.

THANDI: Mr Zuma!

ZUMA: Come, come. Don't be frightened.

THANDI: How dare you!

ZUMA: Don't over-react, Thandi.

THANDI: I am your nurse!

ZUMA: You are like a daughter to me.

THANDI: Nothing else.

ZUMA: I thought we had a special relationship.

THANDI: What do you think it would be like for me if all my patients grabbed me and tried to kiss me!

ZUMA: I am not just any patient.

THANDI: You are just my patient.

KASRILS comes in.

KASRILS: What was he trying to do? Was he molesting you?

ZUMA: Ah, the old man is back. Has your brain calmed down, Indoda?

THANDI: It's alright, Mr Kasrils.

KASRILS: Are you alright?

THANDI: I'm fine.

KASRILS: Keep away from him. Don't go near him or you'll regret it all your life.

ZUMA: The cancer must be leaching into his brain. He is talking like a mad man.

KASRILS: Mind you, his bark is probably much worse than his bite. You have problems with impotence, don't you, spear of the nation.

ZUMA: Let's do the decent thing and ignore him, Thandi.

KASRILS: You've heard of Khwezi, haven't you, Nurse Thandi?

THANDI: Of course. She accused Mr Zuma of raping her. There was a court case. But he was found innocent.

KASRILS: Yes.

ZUMA: Can you truly believe that a man like me, I was in line to be head of the ANC and President of this country, do you believe such a man would rape a young woman?

KASRILS: Tell Nurse Thandi how you knew her.

THANDI: Her father, Judson Kuzwayo, was your comrade. He was a great freedom fighter.

ZUMA: He and I were together on Robben Island. And Mr Kasrils and I knew him in Swaziland. He was our brother.

KASRILS: Her mother, Beauty, was an actress and an ANC fighter.

THANDI: And they had a sweet little girl, Fezekile, known to the world later, when they tried to keep her identity secret, as Khwezi.

KASRILS: Yes. We called her Fezeka. Sweet and smiley, and full of fun and laughter. You remember, Jacob. She looked after us when we were in hiding there for a few days. She used to bring us newspapers, understood not to let anyone know who we were, that we were there. Gave us tea, constantly offering us things to eat. She loved ice cream. Do you remember, Jacob? 'Have some Uncle Jacob, have some Uncle Ronnie'. You eat it, we'd say. We've had ours. 'But maybe you want some more'. She was such a sweet girl. Loving. Trusting.

When she was ten her father, her protector, died.

ZUMA: It was a terrible car accident. To this day no one knows if it was an accident or sabotage.

KASRILS: Being without a father, a protector was a very dangerous thing for a young girl. At thirteen she was raped for the first time.

ZUMA: That's what she said.

THANDI: At thirteen, it is rape!

ZUMA: Ya ya, of course, at thirteen, sure.

KASRILS: After the transition they moved back to South Africa. Life was hard, as it was for so many. She wanted to study abroad. I tried to get her a scholarship.

ZUMA: It was very hard for her. She was HIV positive, you know.

KASRILS: And a lesbian.

ZUMA: Well, so she said.

KASRILS: One day she was invited to the Zumas. She spent a pleasant evening and was invited to stay in the guest room. She went to bed and was half asleep when the door opened.

THANDI: Mr Zuma.

KASRILS: He went in. He sat next to her and spoke gently to her and then hugged her and then started to touch her, much to her distress.

ZUMA: Nonsense.

KASRILS: And then he raped her.

ZUMA: It was not rape. He told her to say it was rape.

KASRILS: She phoned me the next day. Uncle Ronnie, Jacob Zuma has raped me. Her exact words. Not Uncle Jacob. She said, Jacob Zuma has raped me.

THANDI: Why did she phone you?

KASRILS: She wanted to tell me. When there's no witness to a rape, the authorities need to know whether the complainant has confided in anyone.

ZUMA: And you told her to lay a charge.

KASRILS: She had already made up her mind before she
    confided in me.

ZUMA: You told her to lay a charge and she did.

KASRILS: I told her I could not get involved.

THANDI: You said that?!

KASRILS: Not for my sake but for hers. If I had, it would be
    seen as my fight against Zuma. They'll politicise it, I said,
    you would be completely forgotten in the whole thing.
    Airbrushed out. She was quiet for a moment and then
    said calmly, 'it's alright Uncle Ronnie. I understand. I can
    handle this. I'm an adult now'.

    But of course, that didn't stop you. You still called it a
    honey trap.

ZUMA: You went straight to Mbeki.

KASRILS: I did! I said, 'Mr President. There is a monster
    walking this land and his name is Jacob Zuma.'

ZUMA: Thandi, I ask you. What comrade calls another
    comrade a monster?

KASRILS: A comrade who sees a rapist!

    And the ANC supported you. Poor, unfortunate Zuma,
    they said. We all know his incapacity to control his manly
    libido. It was all a bit of a joke.

ZUMA: She enticed me. She appeared as if she wanted sex.
    Often a woman who is not sure of who she is…

THANDI: What every lesbian needs is a proper man to
    satisfy her?

ZUMA: Sometimes they don't know what they want, Thandi, until they experience it with a real man. Women have changed after they've been with me. I am in tune with a woman's movements. I listen to her sounds and I know how to respond, what she needs me to do.

KASRILS: Then he had a shower!

ZUMA: I always take a hot shower after sex.

KASRILS: And told the world having a shower after sex minimised the risk of becoming HIV positive.

THANDI: You risked the lives of hundreds of thousands of innocent victims. Victims of the men who thought if Zuma can shower after sex and be alright, so can I. If Zuma doesn't use a condom, why should I?

ZUMA: I can't be responsible for what everybody does in the bedroom.

KASRILS: And what's worse, you tried to shut her up, to stop her going ahead with the charge, with money which she desperately needed. You got her Aunties, women she'd known all her life, those loyal ANC comrades to go to her, to pressure her and her mother. Don't say anything to harm him Fezeka, tell her Beauty, what it can do to the ANC, to our President in the wings. Take the money and just be quiet. It's what we women have to live with. We all have to put up with it. Why shouldn't you!

THANDI: Fezeka and Beauty didn't take the money. And they did talk. And there was a trial.

ZUMA: And I was found not guilty! It was a fair court case. We're a democracy with separate legislative and judicial powers.

KASRILS: The Afrikaner judge didn't take notice of the experts who spoke about why women sometimes don't shout out.

ZUMA: We had sex. My daughter was in the house. A policeman was outside. Did anyone hear her scream. No! Why? If a woman is raped, she screams! It was consensual.

THANDI: She would not have screamed. You were her malume, her uncle. She would have deferred to you.

KASRILS: The judge dismissed her mother's evidence as incoherent.

ZUMA: Poor Beauty. She is suffering from dementia. You can hardly understand a word the poor woman says.

THANDI: But he allowed evidence about Fezeka's sexual history, the previous rapes and paraded witnesses in court who spoke about having consensual sex with her.

ZUMA: It was relevant.

THANDI: She is allowed to have a sexual history.

KASRILS: And the revelations from Fezeka's own diary. She didn't have a clue how they got it.

THANDI: They stole it.

KASRILS: All of this should have been irrelevant and not allowed in court.

ZUMA: I was the accused. Not the judge. I didn't make the decisions.

KASRILS: 'If you can control your body and your sexual urges, then you are a man, my son.' What? That white, middle class Afrikaner quotes Kipling to you, one of the highest officials in the land, in post-Apartheid South

Africa! How disgraceful! But he who is without shame, finds a remark like that, inconsequential.

THANDI: And the guilty one became Fezeka.

We hear a crowd yelling, Zuma, Zuma, and 'Burn the bitch.'

ZUMA starts to sing the struggle song, 'Umshini Wam – Bring me my machine gun'.

The crowd is ecstatic and ZUMA is the king.

KASRILS and THANDI watch. THANDI is horrified. ZUMA laughs.

THANDI: Fezeka's house was burnt. She and her mother ran away, back into exile. Her life wasn't safe. She moved from job to job. People said she was very good with children. Eventually, they returned home. And when she was forty, Fezeka suddenly died.

ZUMA: How do you know so much about her?

THANDI: We young women know about her. We protest and hold up banners. 'Remember Khwezi'.

Pause.

ZUMA: You are one of them? I would never have believed that of you! You, a Zulu woman. You call me your President and yet you betray me too.

THANDI: Mr Zuma, you are my patient. I think you should both rest now.

She exits.

ZUMA: She feels sorry for me.

KASRILS: I'd say despise, myself.

ZUMA: It's a long time since I've noticed someone feeling sorry for me. The last time was when I was a little boy, walking in Durban after being told to leave my mother, barefoot, threadbare vest, ragged shorts. Tears streaming down my face.

Most people who passed looked away, didn't want to see a little picaninny hungry, thirsty, crying. But an old Indian woman saw me and gave me some pennies. 'Go buy yourself an ice-cream', she said to me.

There was an 'ice-cream boy' on the corner – you remember those, Ronnie, ice-cream boys with their bikes and little ice boxes. I stood in a queue behind a couple of white boys who looked me up and down. I walked away with an eskimo pie and sat on the edge of the pavement with my feet in the street. I ate that ice-cream. And you know what, Ronnie? It made me thirsty and I was still hungry. I should have bought some bread and asked for water. But for five minutes I was the same as every other boy, someone who could buy himself an ice-cream when it was hot and he was upset. Who would have thought that little boy would one day be a guest of the Queen of Great Britain and spend the night in Buckingham Palace.

KASRILS: The big missus. Though the Press was less favourable, shall we say.

Voice over from Press.

PRESS: Jacob Zuma is a sex obsessed bigot with four wives and thirty-five children. So why is Britain fawning over this vile buffoon?

ZUMA: Am I being too sensitive or do you think it's a bit too close to baboon?

KASRILS: Racist bastards.

ZUMA: Ahh, so when the chips are down, you'll still support me, hey Ronnie?

KASRILS: Over the racist *Daily Mail*? Any day. You might be a vile buffoon but you're our vile buffoon. And if anyone's going to say it, it's going to be us.

ZUMA: *(Laughs.)*

KASRILS: It could've been so different. That little boy sitting on the pavement could have grown up to be a great President.

ZUMA: Hai Ronnie. You can't imagine what it's like when everyone turns against you. The reality of everyone who's been your friend, your supporter, your brother, telling you, to leave, to resign. Think of the ANC. Think of your country. And it gets stronger and stronger, more and more nasty, personal, hard, the longer you say, no, I'm staying, I'll fight it out. But then you suddenly find you're alone in the middle of your worst nightmare.

Silence.

ZUMA: You can fight…if you have comrades.

KASRILS: You'll never be President again

ZUMA: Who says?

KASRILS: I do!

ZUMA: You? You're an old man. Nobody's going to listen to you. You're a spent force, a nothing.

KASRILS: I've still got life in me, and I swear, as long as I'm around, I'll fight to make sure

ZUMA: You'll fight? You can't fight anymore, old man.

KASRILS: that you and your cronies are stopped, because those bastards will just continue to rape and plunder this country and all its people after both of us have gone to our graves.

ZUMA: I offered you a chance to get people to listen. But you threw it back in my face.

KASRILS: You should've gone as soon as it became obvious.

ZUMA: Should've. I don't work on should've. The only thing I should've done is punish my enemies and never have allowed my opponents to get on top of me! I should have been a dictator. At least for a day. Think what I could have achieved as a dictator!

KASRILS: Bloody hell!

ZUMA: I don't like this feeling. I won't feel like this. I was the President of this country. I had people fawning over me, begging me, offering me, giving me, wanting me. That is me. Not this.

THANDI enters.

THANDI: Mr Kasrils, I must take some blood.

She sorts him out.

KASRILS: You fucked up this country good and bloody proper! Excuse my language, Nurse. You put it back decades. Do you realise that? You allowed state capture. You bloody enabled it. You made it happen. You appointed useless flunkies to top positions in cabinet and in state enterprises. You sold off our institutions to the highest bidder, often not even the highest, just whoever it was who pulled the strings. Yes Mr Gupta sir, no Mr Gupta sir. It's the same as yes madam, no baas. You never got Apartheid out of you. You just found another baas and let them walk all over you, stamp on you and use you like a common whore.

ZUMA: State capture! What a politically decorated expression that is!

KASRILS: You let them take what they wanted and they cut you a nice slice of ice cream cake that you spread all over your face!

ZUMA: You're wrong! I will do it. I will get back. The people want me. They love me. All Zulus love me. Even if I make a mistake. They forgive me. Look at Nurse Thandi. She understands what I really am.

KASRILS: And what's that?

ZUMA: I'm a simple man.

KASRILS laughs.

ZUMA: Just a simple man.

KASRILS: You're the reality of South Africa.

ZUMA: Yes.

KASRILS: You are the ugly truth that shows itself with every xenophobic outrage, every back hander slipped under the table, every crooked deal. You embody it.

THANDI: I don't want you back.

ZUMA: Of course you do!

THANDI: No. I don't.

ZUMA: Why?

Pause.

THANDI: *(Very quietly.)* You're unworthy.

KASRILS: What?

THANDI: *(Louder.)* You're unworthy and weak.

ZUMA: Weak?! Me. I am a lion!

THANDI: No. You are...a hyena.

ZUMA: But my people love me.

THANDI: Not me.

ZUMA: You carry on loving Mandela. Why not me?

THANDI: You are not Madiba. Madiba is a gentleman and you are a boor. Madiba has one wife who is a lady and he does not try to kiss young women who are repulsed by him.

Madiba had integrity and you have none.

ZUMA: And what would have happened to Madiba if it hadn't been for the likes of Kasrils and me, if we hadn't struggled all our lives for his freedom, and yours too, Thandi.

THANDI: That is history.

KASRILS: History is relevant. You have to remember the past.

THANDI: Oh no sir, we aren't dismissing the past. The past has happened. It is the present that we are locked into. Apartheid is over. We are the post-apartheid generation. We have our own struggles now. We have problems that we feel we carry on our own back because old men and women in power, don't understand our problems. They don't listen to us. Our democracy itself is, I was going to say in intensive care but that would assume there are people treating and caring for it and ensuring it survives, and that's not the case. Mr. Zuma, you and you too Mr Kasrils, are stuck in the past, fighting old battles. And you're not listening to what we have to say. You pretend to listen but it is with only half an ear. You don't understand because either you are damaged or affected by all that you went through, all your struggles and suffering. Young people are frustrated and impatient so they end up rejecting everything. I don't want to burn down libraries because university fees are high, but the truth is your generation only sit up and take note when students go on the rampage. You became complacent in power and you left the people behind. I don't want old-style liberals or radicals or anything else. I don't care if someone says they are a communist or a capitalist. But I do care if they are egotists, or sexist misogynists, or power-crazy people who play the tribal card. I don't really care about black or white, or Zulu or Xhosa or Shangaan or from Cameroon. It all just seems to intrude into everything you do, all the time. What I want is a job and a home and a decent salary. I want education and a better environment and proper transport. I want that for me and I want it for everyone. I want it for all those beggars and babies and children and young people who have nothing. I don't know if that makes me an idealist, but I know I don't want corruption and I don't want inequality. I don't want to be told what I want. And I don't want some old man trying to kiss me.

Pause.

KASRILS: Jacob. If it helps, I'm sorry

ZUMA: Is that the apology, Ronnie?

KASRILS: that it's worked out like this for you. That you stand here alone and shamed.

ZUMA: I don't stand alone Ronnie. It seems I stand again together with you, side by side, both of us together again, being told we are no longer relevant. Do I accept it? Do you?

KASRILS: If we accept it, it means we just stop. I'm only eighty. I've got the rest of my life ahead of me.

ZUMA: Heh heh, Kumalo. That's it, hey! We've got to carry on living.

KASRILS: But in Nkandla, please Jacob. Just you and your wives and your children and your grandchildren. Surely that's enough for you. Go and be a big man with your family. And your cows. You have cows now, not just goats. Let the country be now. Let it recover.

THANDI finishes putting on a plaster/bandage on KASRILS.

THANDI: There you are, Mr Kasrils, that's done. Come now gentlemen. The doctors will be doing their rounds soon. I have to go get your early evening meal. I'm sure I'm right in supposing you won't want any ice cream for dessert?

KASRILS/ZUMA: What!

THANDI: Ha! Got you both!

KASRILS/ZUMA: Nurse Thandi!/Thandi!

THANDI: Course you'll get your ice-cream but no food or even tea after ten. Tomorrow first thing we take your blood and urine samples. Then your medical examinations. Mr Zuma, Mr Kasrils no more debate. Rest time right now!

Pause while KASRILS and ZUMA both collect themselves together.

ZUMA: But I haven't beaten him at chess yet.

KASRILS: Hey you vile buffoon. Do you really think you can beat me at chess?

ZUMA: Look at the mampara. This is what a deluded fool looks like.

KASRILS: Tomorrow?

ZUMA: Tomorrow. I've got to go pee. It might take some time.

As they exit, they look back at each other, and fire imaginary gun shots.

ZUMA: Etwa, etwa.

KASRILS: Etwa, etwa.

BLACK

Printed in the USA
CPSIA information can be obtained
at www.ICGtesting.com
LVHW020958171024
794056LV00004B/1221